Genre Realist

M000289213

Essential Quest...
How are families around the world the same and different?

I'm Down Under

by Parker Wu
illustrated by Louise Ellis

Chapter 1 Goodbye, California

March 1

My mom and I are moving to Australia. Mom has a new job in Sydney. She gave me this journal so I can write what happens.

I don't know what to think. I'm excited about moving to a new country and learning about a new culture. But I'm also nervous. "Don't worry, Ella," Mom said to me. "Everything will be fine."

But what if I don't make any new friends? It doesn't seem fair that I have to leave my friends in California.

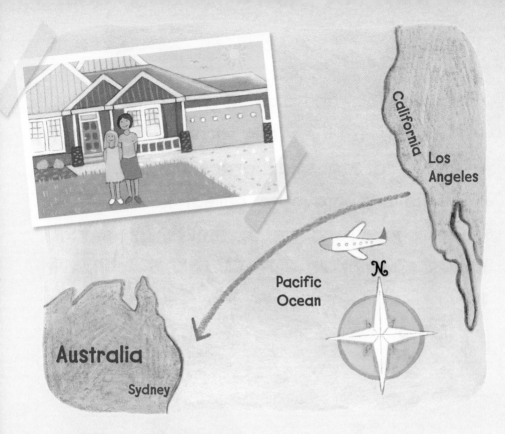

March 17

Our new house in Sydney is a lot like our old house in California. I can see the Pacific Ocean from my bedroom window. It's the same ocean that you see in California. We're just on the other side of it.

Today I found out that Australia is sometimes called Down Under. That's because it's way down below the equator.

March 18

Today Mom and I went shopping. We walked to the dairy around the corner. That's a small grocery store. They don't have my favorite cereal here. I don't recognize a lot of the things in the stores. I'm not so sure I'm going to like it here.

Mom bought me something to eat called a sausage roll. It has meat inside pastry. It wasn't quite the same as having a hot dog, but it was still pretty yummy!

Chapter 2 New Friends

March 20

Today I made a new friend. Her name is Kate, and she lives next door. She and her mom came over to say hello.

Tomorrow will be my first day at school. I'm in the same class as Kate. She offered to walk to school with me. Maybe I won't be so nervous with her there.

March 21

It felt so strange to wear a uniform to school today. Kate says I'll get used to it. I like our teacher, Mrs. Wong. She took me aside to make sure I was feeling all right.

There's a map of Australia in the classroom. Mrs. Wong put a map of the United States next to it. She asked me to show the class where California is.

At lunch, I met Kate's friends, and we played a game of netball. It's a bit like basketball, but the rules are different. You can't bounce the ball. If you do, the other team gets the ball. It took me a long time to learn that rule!

March 22

It's hard getting used to the different words and sayings here. They also speak English with a different accent. Sometimes I can't understand what people are saying, even though we speak the same language. But Kate tells me what they mean. Kate can understand my accent because she watches American shows on TV!

American English	Australian English
gas	petrol
cookie	biscuit
faucet	tap
apartment	flat
flashlight	torch
candy	sweets

Chapter 3 / Two Homes

March 23

Today I went over to Kate's house after school. Her mom made us a sandwich with a thick, brown paste inside. It looked like jelly, but it tasted salty. Everyone here loves it, but I like peanut butter much better.

I remembered how I used to share peanut butter sandwiches with my friend Michelle in California. That made me feel homesick all of a sudden. Kate was really nice to me when she saw I was sad.

Then Kate and I hung out in her room. She has a guinea pig named Henry. He scurries out of sight when someone comes in the room. Kate has posters of famous netball players on her walls. She gave me one for my room. That made me feel a lot better.

March 26

Tomorrow we're going to Kate's house for dinner. They have invited us to a barbie, which is short for a barbecue. Kate's mom asked us to bring an American dish, so we made an apple pie.

March 27

When we arrived at Kate's, we saw a huge cake on the table. It looked amazing. Kate told me that it's called a pavlova. I was worried. What if they didn't like our apple pie?

Kate's dad grilled a huge pile of sausages. We wrapped the sausages in bread. Then we put tomato sauce on top. Australian tomato sauce is just like our ketchup. The barbecue tasted great.

Then it was time for dessert. Kate had helped her mom make the pavlova. It is a light, sweet cake topped with whipped cream and fruit.

I felt really nervous when they started to eat the apple pie, but they liked it. "It's so good!" Kate said.

"Tastes great," said Kate's mom.

I suddenly felt very hungry! The pavlova tasted delicious. Kate tried to plead for another slice of apple pie, but her mom said she wanted to save some.

March 30

I emailed my grandma today about our life in Australia. Mom says that we can visit California later this year and stay with her.

I miss my grandma, and I miss my old friends. But I like my new friends here too. I guess I have two homes now — one on each side of the Pacific Ocean!

Respond to Reading

Summarize

Use important details to help you summarize *I'm Down Under*.

Character	Setting	Events

Text Evidence

1. How do you know that *I'm Down Under* is realistic fiction? Genre

2. What is unusual about the setting for the story? Use story details to support your answer. Character, Setting, Events

3. Use what you know of root words to figure out the meaning of *looked* on page 13. Root Words

4. Write about how the author shows you what Ella is like. Write About Reading

Compare Texts

Read more about the dessert called *pavlova*.

Perfect Pavlova

In Australia and New Zealand, some people call pavlova the national dessert. People often have pavlova on special occasions or holidays, but it can be served all year round.

(t) Yvette Cardozo/Photolibrary/Getty Images, (bkgd) Nic Taylor/Photodisc/Getty Images, (l) Zoonar GmbH/Alamy, (r) Bon Appetit/Alamy

Pavlova is a sweet, light cake. It is made from whipped egg whites and sugar. First, the mixture is baked and then cooled. Next, it is covered with whipped cream. Finally, it is topped with kiwis, berries, and other fruit. The cake is crispy on the outside and soft inside.

Why is this cake called pavlova? A long time ago, there was a famous Russian ballet dancer named Anna Pavlova. Some people called her the greatest ballerina of her time. One story says that a New Zealand chef created the dessert and named it after the ballerina. Another story says an Australian chef created it. No matter who made it first, many people enjoy eating it!

Make Connections

How are Kate's and Ella's families alike? **Essential Question**

What are some things in Australia that are different from your country? Text to Text

(t) Yvette Cardozo/PhotoLibrary/Getty Images, (bkgd) Nic Taylor/Photodisc/Getty Images, (inset) Time & Life Pictures/Getty Images.

Focus on
Social Studies

Purpose To compare ways we celebrate special occasions

What to Do

Step 1 ▶ Talk with a partner about an occasion your family celebrates, like a holiday or a birthday.

Step 2 ▶ Draw a picture showing how you celebrate. Include people you celebrate with and things that you do.

Step 3 ▶ Write a sentence about the things you do.

Step 4 ▶ Share your picture with your partner. Talk about ways you each celebrate. How are your celebrations alike or different?